G000298956

CONDUCT WHICH HONOURS GOD?

The question of
homosexuality

Simon Vibert

Fellowship of Word and Spirit

ORTHOS

is a series of booklets from
Fellowship of Word and Spirit
Biblical Theology for the 21st Century
Series Editor: Lance Bidewell

© Simon Vibert 1995, 2003
First published in 1995 by Fellowship of Word and Spirit. This edition published in 2003.
The right of Simon Vibert to be identified as the author of this work has been asserted by him in accordance with the Copyright, Designs and Patents Act 1988.

All rights reserved. No part of this publication may be reproduced or stored or transmitted by any means or in any form, electronic or mechanical, including photocopying, recording, or in any information storage or retrieval system, without permission, which should be sought from the publisher, Fellowship of Word and Spirit.

The views expressed in *Orthos* are those of the author and do not necessarily represent those of the Trustees or Council of Fellowship of Word and Spirit.

All biblical quotations are taken from the NIV, unless otherwise stated.

Further copies of *Orthos* and information about the Fellowship may be obtained from:
Fellowship of Word and Spirit, 86 All Hallows Road, Bispham, Blackpool, Lancashire FY2 OAY, England
Web site: www.fows.org

Typesetting by Amanda Scott
Printed in Great Britain by
Print-out, Histon, Cambridge CB4 4JD

ISBN 1 874694 09 5

Foreword to the first edition

This is a stimulating booklet which I am glad to commend.

It comes in two halves which make up a satisfying whole. In the first part, Simon Vibert extends the parameters of the biblical debate about homosexuality in several refreshing ways. Instead of a narrow concentration on the morality of same-sex acts, he shifts the spotlight to focus on the alternative lifestyle which Scripture commends as honouring to God. And rather than a straightforward analysis of the relevant biblical texts, he urges us to explore their interpretation within a larger doctrinal matrix of creation, fall, redemption and eschatology. Every reader will not agree with every detail, but there is more than enough to spur fresh and purposeful exploration of the Bible's teaching.

It was a master-stroke to complement the clear-cut veto on homosexual behaviour which emerges from part one with the record of the interview with Martin Hallett, director of the True Freedom Trust, which makes up part two. Here, with great sensitivity, the outline of an alternative, biblical lifestyle is pieced together empathetically – an approach far more helpful than a cold demand for abstinence.

Some responses to other people's work are dull and sterile. This one does not belong in that category. The author is the first to admit that he has not produced a full critique of Michael Vasey's Grove booklet. That debate will doubtless continue. But we can all be grateful to Simon Vibert for redirecting our attention from culture to creation.

David Field
Church Pastoral Aid Society

Introduction to the second edition

I wrote *Conduct Which Honours God?* in 1995. Since then, the late Michael Vasey published his book *Strangers and Friends.*[1] This has proved to be an important contribution, not least because, as tutor of an evangelical theological college, he proposed a major revision of evangelical perspectives on homosexuality in the church.

At the end of 1995 the St Andrew's Day Statement was published, and later responded to by a wide spectrum of authors in the book *The Way Forward?*[2]

Things have moved quite quickly this year, and two of the essays in that book, 'Christian Same-Sex Partnerships' by Jeffrey John and 'Knowing Myself in Christ' by Rowan Williams, have proved to be very significant.

The appointment of Dr Rowan Williams in 2002 to be Archbishop of Canterbury has caused a stir among mainstream evangelicals, not least because of his views on the subject of homosexuality (as laid out in *The Way Forward?* and also *The Body's Grace*[3]).

When Dr Jeffrey John accepted Bishop Richard Harries's offer to be the next Bishop of Reading, there was considerable concern expressed in the diocese of Oxford, and indeed across the worldwide Anglican Communion.[4]

Dr John's preferment came hard on the heels of the June 2002 decision by the Anglican diocese of New Westminster to authorize a liturgy to bless same-sex unions. English evangelicals swiftly brought pressure to bear on Jeffrey John and Rowan Williams to call for the withdrawal of Jeffrey John as the next Bishop of Reading. Despite Jeffrey John's assurance that he was no longer in a sexually active relationship with his partner of 27 years, he has seen no need to repent of his former sexual relationship and continues to stand by his teaching in *The Way Forward?*

The Anglican Communion is still coming to terms with both Jeffrey John's withdrawal and Canon Gene Robinson's acceptance of the offer of episcopal office in the diocese of New Hampshire, USA. The latter's position is more worrying for the Anglican Communion, because Canon Robinson shows no sign of repentance and, in a recent article in the *Kansas City Star* (17th July 2003), sees no need either to withdraw his acceptance or to leave his partnership with Mark Andrew, with whom, after divorcing his wife, he has been since 1989. Canon Robinson believes that evangelicals have misunderstood scriptural teaching on the subject of faithful homosexual love, and challenges evangelicals to meet him and his partner so that they can see the genuineness of their relationship.

It is in this climate that I have made a few changes to *Conduct Which Honours God?* The principle changes have been:

- An update of my writing on Michael Vasey to include the new material from his book *Strangers and Friends*.

- I have also updated the 'against nature' argument in Romans 1 to take on board some of the recent writing on it, including, most helpfully, Robert Gagnon's book *The Bible and Homosexual Practice*.[5]

- A new section which looks at the now current discussion, 'faithful, covenanted partnerships', especially focusing on the two chapters by Rowan Williams and Jeffrey John in *The Way Forward?*

- Finally, a new section which includes 'sound-bite' answers to popular objections to the way in which the homosexuality debate has been handled. It is commonly objected, for example, that those who wear poly-cotton shirts and eat prawns have no right to appeal to Old Testament texts as the basis of current moral law; or, some argue, Jesus never said anything on this subject, and neither should we. Much of this debate is carried on at the popular, sound-bite level, and I hope that the final section will help the reader to answer the popular argument clearly.

Obviously this booklet cannot be, and does not intend to be, exhaustive. Perhaps, as never before, evangelical Christians have come under fierce attack from liberals within the church and from the news media in our culture. Evangelicals are described as 'hardline', 'intolerant' and even, atrociously, as the 'evangelical Taliban'. There has never been a more important time 'to speak the truth in love'. My hope is that this booklet will assist us do *both*: speak truth and show love. In order for that to happen, we need to be aware of how much the culture and prevailing attitudes have dominated our thinking about this and most other issues. We need to know the Truth! But, we need to be aware of *how* we are heard, and, as ever, to allow ourselves to accommodate our language and practice to be as generously loving with the message of the gospel as we can.

Simon Vibert
September 2003

The Revd Dr Simon Vibert is vicar of St Luke's Church, Wimbledon Park.

Conduct which honours God?
The question of homosexuality

My concern is that we answer the question: 'What lifestyle and conduct are honouring to God?' The current debate in the Church of England has surrounded the attitude which the church should have towards those who commit homosexual acts. As I shall argue a little later, the testing of godliness by conduct is biblical and needs to happen (e.g. 1 Tim. 3; 1 Pet. 4-5). However, there seems to be a fear among evangelicals that it is too messy to discuss in detail how, for example, someone with a homosexual orientation may live in a way which honours God. For many homosexuals, their sexuality is expressed in a cultural lifestyle with its own language, dress, social life and 'world-view'. For homosexuals, as for heterosexuals, the recognition and expression of their sexuality is much broader than genital acts. What, then, does the Bible have to say to those who, under God, seek to sustain a Christ-honouring lifestyle?

The interview with Martin Hallett at the end of this booklet shows how one thoughtful Christian seeks to live out his sexuality in a celibate lifestyle. Martin would endorse the traditional condemnation of homosexual acts, but would appeal to evangelical Christians to understand how what we are saying is interpreted by those who are seeking to live biblically. All too often our pro-family approach has the effect of marginalizing those who are celibate, widowed, separated or divorced. In other words, some of the contemporary assumptions relating to what is a godly lifestyle do need to be challenged for having more to do with modern – largely middle-class – culture than the Bible.

I would wish to avoid two prevalent approaches to the issue of homosexuality, which may be found within the wider church. The first is sometimes mistakenly labelled as the 'pastoral approach'. The assumption is made that caring, loving, compassionate gay people are fellow humans loved by God who need to be integrated into the Christian community. Those involved in a gay lifestyle have sometimes been socially ostracized and been victims of prejudice and hate campaigns. I have heard thoughtful Christians remark that when they have seen the love between a caring partner and a gay lover dying of AIDS, they have witnessed a 'Christian' love and godliness which should be endorsed by the church. The difficulty I have with this supposedly pastoral approach to the debate, is that we are not being pastoral if we are not being biblical. Indeed love itself, as we shall see later, is something which needs to be defined by the Bible. Nobody doubts that Canon Jeffrey John nor Canon Gene Robinson are genuinely likeable, articulate and winsome people. However, Christian ethicists have rightly encouraged us to have a certain objectivity in our discussions. We show clearer pastoral concern when we see the issues for what they are, rather than through the personalities who hold them.

However, I would also wish to avoid 'homophobia'. Although I have heard Christians who argue that they are happy to use this word to express biblical intolerance of homosexuality, I am not convinced that it reflects a biblical approach to dealing with any individual who is made in the image of God. Because I believe that we are living in critical times in the defining of Christ-honouring conduct, and because the militant campaigns to endorse an unbiblical approach to the issue of homosexuality are having some 'success', there is a danger that I speak in a way which offends the Christian brother or sister struggling with their sexuality, yet seeking to live in a Christ-honouring way. For example, when I use the words 'sexually deviant' in this booklet, I do so recognizing that there are many forms of sexual deviance other than homosexuality (although I do believe that this sin is more intolerable than some heterosexual sins).

Consequently, the first task is to turn to the Bible, for here we learn godly compassion without sacrificing convictions about holiness and truth. We cannot arrive at some conclusions in this area without first dealing with the biblical material. It can not be assumed that there is universal agreement upon key texts (such as Genesis 19; Romans 1: 18ff.).

THE BIBLE AND THE GAY DEBATE

This booklet began as a talk given to a clergy conference entitled: 'Should the Church be Silent?'. A strange question, perhaps, given that in 1994 and early 1995 the church hit media headlines for nothing much other than the issue of homosexuality.[6] Indeed, in 2003, the British media has had endless coverage of the subject. And, as I mention above, evangelicals have been caricatured as being archaic and unloving. For this very reason, perhaps, we need greater courage to restate views which put us so clearly at odds with the view of the dominant culture.

My purpose is to continue to debate the issue. Although there is talk by conservative evangelicals of a 'watershed' over this matter of the acceptability of homosexual conduct, the issue is bigger than this. Admittedly we may only judge *conduct*, but the Bible itself regards godliness as being bigger than our actions. However, the reason for my initial conference title was partly in response to some correspondence in the church press, one letter being printed as follows:

> I cannot believe that a Christian newspaper could run such misguided and uninformed dribble on such an important issue facing human beings and the church as homosexuality …
>
> Our Lord Jesus said absolutely nothing on the subject of homosexuality – he did say plenty on divorce and look at the ease in which people in high places bend the 'rules'! You state that 'Jesus took the Scriptures as his authority'. You appear to forget that Jesus needed no 'authority'. He was the Word and the Word was God.

The Anglican Church minus the contribution of gay and lesbian Christians would be a sorry sight.[7]

Some of the controversy within the Church of England has centred on the teaching of Michael Vasey, who was tutor at Cranmer Hall, Durham. In *Evangelical Christians and Gay Rights* he argues:

> 'Straight' Christians would be wise to keep silent [over the gay debate] until they have, for example, personally bought and read a responsible paper like the *Gay Times* for a year.[8]

The implication is that we are ignorant and unable to enter the debate until we have fully appreciated the contemporary stand of advocates of 'gay rights'.[9] No evangelical is going to disagree with John Stott's belief that 'double listening' needs to take place if we are to bring the 'ancient word to the modern world'.[10] But we need to be clear that Stott does not thereby assume that the message is shaped or moulded by the modern world: rather that, through hearing where our audience is, we speak in such a way as to ensure that we are heard, and that we empathize with our listeners.[11] But to assume that I am disqualified to speak in the debate until I have spent one year absorbing the material of the gay movement is absurd.

> ... evangelical campaigns have included no recognition of the lived experience of gay people or of their attempt to sustain ordinary life in the midst of hostility, misrepresentation and even violence.[12]

In *Strangers and Friends*, Vasey wrestles with the question of how the church is to come to terms with the gay identity. He begins by giving us his hermeneutical framework by way of analogy with what the Bible has to say about cars. In answering the question about the place of cars in God's economy, a few related questions need to be asked of the Bible. There are biblical theological issues concerning the doctrines of creation and fall in terms of creativity (including the making of cars) and human fallenness (relating to the proud fallen attitude towards cars). An alternative approach is to find cultural equivalents which would raise questions about mobility, technology, ambition.[13] When it comes to assessing what the Bible has to say about homosexuality, we live in a cultural context which is as alien to the Bible's teaching on the offence of perverted sex in a cultic setting, as the motor car is to methods of transport in the Bible. In other words, Vasey argues, the modern gay movement is unanticipated by the Bible writers. The only way to analyse it is to find cultural equivalents to homosexuality which 'is itself a complex cultural phenomenon that has to be seen as a form of same-sex desire mediated through concepts, social arrangements and bodily symbolism that are shared with the rest of society'.[14] Analogies are drawn between the biblical approach used by evangelicals to sustain an argument in favour of the abolition of slavery, and the cultural arguments used to support the use of contraception.

Conduct Which Honours God?

I mention this because I remain concerned that the analysis of ethical conduct may not be undertaken without a biblical framework in place first. What, for example, does Vasey mean by 'gay people'? Does he mean those who have such an orientation but have chosen to live a celibate life? Or does he mean those who are practising homosexuals (inside or outside a 'stable' relationship)? Because, as we shall see, analysing our culture within a biblical framework will mean that some distinctions need to be made (see for example 1 Cor. 5:9-11; 6:9-11). Similarly, the 'ordinary life' Vasey refers to can only be defined by biblical expectations, not by predominant behaviour patterns in contemporary culture. So what is the function of Scripture in this debate?

The question is not whether we are saying anything, but whether we have anything to say! It is true that there are those who deny that there are any instances in the Bible where homosexuality is actively condemned,[15] and this poses questions of exegesis. More sharply, the recent discussions have surrounded whether the Bible has anything to say about the modern debate. Michael Vasey spoke in terms of the modern gay scene being 'unanticipated by the Bible writers'. Similarly, Rowan Williams states:

> If the Bible is very clear — as I think it is — that a heterosexual indulging in homosexual activity for the sake of variety and gratification is not following the will of God, does that automatically say that that is the only sort of homosexual activity there could ever be? My personal conclusion is that I can see a case for acknowledging faithful same-sex relationships.[16]

This means that the hermeneutical issue is sharply focused around the 'new hermeneutic'. There are 'Two Horizons' (If I may borrow Anthony Thiselton's phrase), that of the ancient text and that of the modern interpreter.[17] Modern hermeneutics recognizes that 'historical conditioning is two-sided: the modern interpreter, no less than the text, stands in a given historical context and tradition'.[18] The interrelationship between text and interpretation gives rise to what is known as the 'hermeneutical circle'.

So we need to ask: How does what was said then (at the time of the writing of the Bible) apply to now, the time of applying the Bible in contemporary culture? This issue is complicated by the uncertainty created by postmodern thinking. The meaning of any text is being reduced to subjectivism, or the collective mind of the modern church community, divorced from the intention of the writer. Meaning is defined by the reader, not the writer. The significance of postmodernist hermeneutics is very evident in this debate. David Wells comments:

> ... the significance of this shift in the source of meaning ... is that it aims a blow at the entire Western academic tradition in which it has always been assumed that although all words have ranges of meaning, good authors also know how to limit for the reader what possibilities exist in any given passage. If the only meaning in a text is that which

any particular community wants to provide, then what is normative in language, as well as in life, has been destroyed.[19]

It is popular to accuse evangelicals of blinkered conservatism in this debate, but, we can all be blind to the influence of current trends, and we need to be as aware of this in the area of hermeneutics as in any other. If part of the task of modern interpretation is to see the meaning in any particular culture, then the first task of the biblical interpreter must be to see how the teaching was interpreted in a first-century community. It is a sad trend in modernity that we assume that we know better than every preceding generation. In their challenging critique of modern evangelicalism entitled *No God but God*, by O. Guinness and J. Steel, T. Oden refers to this trend as '[a] debilitating amnesia … about [our] roots in classical orthodoxy.'[20]

One result of this hermeneutical confusion is that it is not possible to assume agreement about key texts in the homosexuality debate. Michael Vasey rather dismisses the 'six or seven knock down arguments' and concludes that they have nothing to say to the modern debate.[21] The uncertainty about the clarity of the Bible on contemporary key issues means that we have to try to address the hermeneutical issue first. If we cannot first agree upon *how* the Bible speaks, the value of debating interpretative details from individual texts is limited. What follows in this booklet assumes that the reader is in agreement with how we approach the text. Central to this assumption is the conviction that our first task is to try to arrive at the authorial intent in the central biblical passages. It may be that the hermeneutical debates remain unsettled in your mind. In which case, before proceeding with the ensuing line of argument, you may wish to follow up some of the preceding footnotes.

In the next section we shall look at a few of the key passages which deal with the issues of homosexuality, even while conceding that there are others who have written much more extensively and adequately on the subject.[22] From this framework we may then turn in our second section to the issue of lifestyle and conduct.

BUILDING A BIBLICAL FRAMEWORK

One of the most hotly disputed texts in this debate is Romans 1:18-32, so it is important that we understand the passage from the context of Romans 1. It is significant in our task of building a biblical structure that we appreciate that the book of Romans is the closest we have to a systematizing of Paul's thought, and in itself provides the framework for understanding God's relationship to his world.

The thesis of Romans is found in 1:16f. 'The revelation of righteousness in the gospel of Jesus Christ' is the main theme of this letter. Just as the universal way of righteousness is through Christ, so the effect of sin and God's judgement upon it is also universal (1:18ff.). Paul moves from the condemnation by God of the Gentile world (those with the eloquent, but stifled, revelation of creation and conscience) to the particular revelation to God's people, the Jews, who through the law should have been conscious of their need of another way of righteousness. The conclusion in 3:20-23 is that all humankind stands condemned before God. God sent Christ to be the means of justification for both Jew and Gentile. Paul first deals with the forensic problem of the unrighteousness of the Jew and Gentile before a Holy God (3:20-5:21), then with the implications of justification in terms of the indwelling life of the Holy Spirit, the process of mortification of sin and sanctification (5:22-8:39). A discussion on the place of ethnic Israel in God's providence follows in chapters 9-11. Chapters 12 and following deal with the practical outworking of the life dedicated to God in terms of believers' relationships with one another; their relationships with non-believers; with the State; and all this in the context of the mandate of Christian love. John Stott helpfully calls this: 'the will of God for changed relationships.'[23] Paul's teaching concerning a changed lifestyle follows his explanation of God's good creative plans which, having been spoiled by sin, are now being rebuilt in Christ.

Although it is not right to call the epistle a systematic theology (Paul was writing in an historical setting to the Church of Rome which he had not yet visited), the Reformers from Melanchton onwards recognized the comprehensive nature of Paul's treatment of the doctrine of God, human sinfulness, and the provision of redemption and renewal in the cross of Jesus Christ. Romans provides a key theological orientation to the discussion of any ethical issue, homosexuality included. T.F.Torrance is surely right to point out that it was more than a coincidence that the second edition of the *Institutes* (Calvin's major theological work) and Calvin's first commentary (on the book of Romans) came out in the same year (1536).[24] In his *Introduction to the Epistle to the Romans*, Calvin argues:

> ... that when any one gains a knowledge of this epistle, he has an entrance opened to him to all the most hidden treasures of Scripture ... The whole epistle is so methodical, that even from its very beginning it is framed according to the rules of art.[25]

The intention of the *Institutes* was 'to provide a simple form of instruction in the Christian way of life'.[26] And so Calvin's structure in the *Institutes* reflected a similar pattern to the outline of the epistle to the Romans, revealing Calvin's concern that the method of teaching Scripture was tied to the message.[27] Just as in the *Epistle to the Romans*, the *Institutes* move from

> the knowledge of God the Creator, to the knowledge of God the Redeemer, to the way of grace in Christ, to the means of grace.

It is from this biblical-theological orientation of creation, fall, redemption and eschatology, and ethics, that we shall approach our subject. Paul's approach to the subject of homosexuality was born out of such a theology. In a similar way, our interpretation of key texts will be shaped by whatever theological framework we bring to the reading of these passages. In other words, we see our first task as being to rebuild a theological framework. Reader, please bear with me as I restate what for many people will be elementary Reformed presuppositions, but it is precisely because they are no longer universally recognized that they need restatement.

1 Creation

Genesis 1 affirms both men and women as being equal in the sight of God, made by him, for him (v.27), and both made in the image of God. They have the joint responsibility of ruling over the created order. And only through procreation will the earth be filled with more human beings made in the likeness of God (an image which, though badly marred by the Fall, nevertheless is not completely obliterated; this is implied by 5:1ff.). It is important that the modern church remembers the biblical teaching that one is not incomplete if one does not get married or have children, or die a virgin! The Bible has no small amount to say to the widow, the orphan, the eunuch and the single person.[28] Genesis 1:26f. refers to our ontological wholeness being made in the likeness of God. Human beings are complete without being married (as of course was the perfect human being Jesus Christ). In the realm of economic relationships the function of the 'one flesh' is to provide the natural relationship for fulfilling sex (as praised in the Song of Solomon) and the context and climate for raising children.

Genesis 2 deals more thoroughly with the complementary roles of male and female as husband and wife (see 2:18ff.). At least three conclusions can be drawn:
* Provision for human loneliness is met in male/female relationships.
* Woman is made like man, to *complement* man.
* Marriage is instituted as the norm (v.24). The context of this verse indicates that the 'one flesh' unit is first an indivisible *social* unit, and secondly a *sexual* union ('Leaving and Cleaving', as the Anglican *Book of Common Prayer* puts it).

2 Fall

In Genesis 3 we notice that at least part of the rebellion which led to the rupturing of the perfect harmony that existed between God and humankind was centred on a conflict between the sexes. We also observe that part of the judgement upon that rebellion was tension between men and women (e.g. 3:16f.).

The most detailed example of the fallenness of human sexuality is found in Genesis 19. So great was the sin of Sodom and Gomorrah that Abraham's pleading in prayer did not have the effect of saving the city, but only the one righteous family of Lot (see 18:16ff.). Lot offers hospitality to the two heavenly messengers arriving late in the town of Sodom, rather than leave them to a vulnerable overnight stay in the town square. Men of the town called to Lot: 'Where are the men who came to you tonight? Bring them out to us so that we can have sex with them' (v.5, NIV). Failing to placate them, Lot offered his two virgin daughters instead, and was himself only saved from the ranting crowd by the intervention of his two visitors.

In English usage, 'sodomy' refers to anal intercourse. The etymology of the word reflects the widely-held conviction that this text deals with homosexual rape of the grossest form. God judges homosexual sex to be abhorrent and worthy of the severest punishment. The sheer fact that the offer of sex with Lot's daughters did not satisfy, indicates the level to which the people's sexual depravity had fallen.[29]

However, this traditional interpretation of the sin of Sodom and Gomorrah (and indeed the similar sin in Judges 19) has come under serious review following the publication of Derrick Sherwin Bailey's book *Homosexuality and the Western Christian Tradition.*[30] His argument is that the sin of Sodom was not homosexuality but breaking the cultural customs of hospitality. An alien in a foreign city, such as Lot, should not be entertaining visitors in this way: he was exceeding his rights as an alien. Bailey's thesis has become so well known that the limited grounds upon which it is based have often been forgotten.

The argument centres upon verse 5: 'Bring them out so we can (συγγενώμεθα, LXX; know, KJV; have sex, NIV) with them.' Bailey argues that the word 'know' is not meant in the sexual sense. David Field in *The Homosexual Way - a Christian Approach*, points out that from a linguistic point of view this involves

> taking the word 'know' in completely different senses in the space of four verses (Gen. 19:5, 8; Judg. 19:22, 25). Much more seriously, it fails to explain why on each occasion the host replied to a request for a formal introduction by offering his daughter for sexual abuse — and why the visitor's concubine was so severely assaulted at Gibeah. It also raises serious doubts about the interpretation the New Testament puts on the punishment of Sodom (in Jude 7).[31]

Indeed, having established the fact that this passage is referring to homosexual rape, the severity of judgement (see Gen.13:13; 18:20f.; 19:25, and of course Jude 7) indicates just how strongly the sin is viewed. Admittedly this does not yet answer the problem the modern debate raises concerning the legitimacy of 'stable and loving' homosexual relationships. The Bible does not appear to make a distinction between 'perversion' — behaviour that is unnatural and debasing — and 'inversion', which is perceived to be a natural expression of sexuality for a homosexual. To be fair, most homosexuals would find the scenario of Genesis 19 as abhorrent as would most heterosexuals.

However, we must also be careful when we use the contemporary recognition of these distinctions between what some would perceive to be natural orientation, and perversion, to allow liberties which were never intended by the Old Testament text. For example, in Leviticus 18 a list of eighteen unlawful sexual relationships is outlined. Included in this list is: 'Do not lie with a man as one lies with a woman; that is detestable' [32] (18:22, NIV). The motive for these laws is at least partly that the people of Israel are to be distinct in their conduct, as opposed to the promiscuous and idolatrous nations which they are about to inhabit (18:24ff.). 'To lie with' clearly includes the idea of sexual relations. It may be that the writer of Leviticus does not want to exalt homosexuality by using the phrase 'sexual relations' as he has with preceding deviant sexual behaviour. It is possible that 'to lie with', whilst including sexual relationships, may also have the idea of our English phrase 'make your bed and lie in it', in terms of cohabiting. This goes against what God dictates as being natural, and hence is in a different category from the wearing of garments made of different cloths (Lev. 19:20), which is culturally bound (see 'Answering the Popular Arguments', below).

We need, now, to turn to one of the central passages in the debate, Romans 1:18ff. For in this passage, as we have already mentioned, Paul begins his theological framework by stating precisely what behaviour it is that is so abhorrent to God. We shall see that there is more implied about this sin than perhaps at first meets the eye.

a) Paul's argument

It is important that we appreciate the logical progression of Paul's argument in this passage.

i) The wrath of God is his sustained holy revulsion at unrighteousness and unholiness (ungodly conduct and moral infidelity), universally manifested towards those who have suppressed the truth.

ii) This truth is 'plain', in the revelation manifested in the created world, but has been suppressed (κατέχειν).[33] Men and women 'know' (γνόντες) God, but have failed to glorify him or give thanks to him. In other words, their problem is not lack of knowledge but lack of acknowledgment.

iii) The result of this vain thinking is that we worship vainly. Idolatry in the Old Testament is sometimes shortened to the worship of 'vanities' because of the emptiness and insubstantial nature of idols.

iv) As a result of the suppression of the knowledge of God which is plain to all people, humankind, rather than worshipping their Creator, instead worship the creation. The result is the judgement of God. Vain worship reaps a vain lifestyle. Futile thinking reaps futility in every walk of life.

v) Three times Paul uses the phrase: 'God gave them over', emphasizing a downward spiral of degradation as God allows us to reap the consequences of our sin. It is important to appreciate that the disordering of human relationships is part of the judgement of God upon the sin of failing to acknowledge him. In other words, religious and cultural disintegration is an evidence that God is judging our worst sin, the failure to love God with all our heart, soul, mind and strength.

b) The downward spiral

i) Heterosexual relationships are degraded (v.24)

It seems to me that the first stage in the degrading consequences of our sin is in the twisting of natural relationships — between men and women. We have already noticed this as a consequence of the Fall (Gen. 3:16). Ἀκαθαρσία refers to 'uncleanness' (KJV), the moral defilement that comes from breaking the law of God. The first stage in the breakdown of the society is manifested in the breakdown of a biblically defined distinction in male/female relationships.

ii) Open homosexuality is practised (v.26ff.)

The two words 'unnatural' and 'indecent' indicate that Paul sees these relationships as being *perverted* (Πλάνη).[34] Paul indicates that this is a stage worse than the abuse of the natural gift of sexuality. However, there are those who do not believe that Paul is blankly condemning the homosexuality which would be prevalent in the degraded Roman Empire.

This brings us to the important issue of what constitutes 'unnatural'. When Paul refers to sins against nature, is he referring to human nature (which may have different cultural expressions) or are there criteria which dictate a universal timelessness to what is 'natural'?

Michael Vasey writes:

> 'Nature' to Paul is not simply what biology dictates; it is a construct of biology and culture. This is not to argue that there is no mandate written into creation but it makes it harder to identify what this mandate is.[35]

He goes on to take issue with Aquinas' famous list of 'sins against nature': bestiality, homosexual sex, non-procreative heterosexual sex, masturbation. 'The "sins against nature" are more serious than sexual sins within the natural order such as adultery, seduction, and rape'.[36] For Vasey, 'natural' is culturally defined. He uses the acceptance of contraception as an example which has:

> profoundly affected the whole mood of modern society. It is through this, rather than through any 'permissive' conspiracy in the 1960s, that new attitudes to sexuality have come. It has ushered in new perceptions of the 'natural'. Changes have included a positive attitude to sexual pleasure, a rediscovery of feminine sexuality, and significant alterations to the meaning of 'family' and of sexual intercourse itself ... bodily sexual acts appear to derive much of their meaning from the symbolic world of the society in which they occur.[37]

It needs to be said that much of the church's teaching about what constitutes 'sins against nature' has had only a tenuous link with Scripture. However, the logic of Romans 1, verses 24, 26 and 28, indicates that we are looking at increasing degrees of degradation. Heterosexual sins are the first stage in the development (v.24f.) Paul moves in verses 26 to 28 to new lows in conduct, for these are not 'natural' (φυσικην).

The question is: Is a person with only homosexual desires acting *against* (or *contrary to)*[38]*nature* when he/she has same-sex relationships? Or is that person merely expressing his/her nature.

Jeffrey John writes: 'When Paul argues that homosexuality is "against nature" he does not only mean that it is against the order of nature itself, but that it is against the person's own nature.' Apparently, because Paul did not recognize a natural homosexual orientation, homosexuality is to be understood as perverted behaviour by naturally oriented heterosexuals.[39]

This may be deduced from the phrase 'give up' or 'exchange' (v.26f.).

> Paul must believe that homosexuals wilfully choose their unnatural perversion in the same way that he must believe that idolaters wilfully suppress the truth about God that must be known to them from observing creation. Otherwise, as he says, God would not be just in his condemnation, and Paul could not say they are without excuse (vv. 19-20).[40]

In the same collection of essays, Rowan Williams makes a similar deduction concerning our advances in understanding about homosexual orientation. He asks:

> Is the mere fact of homosexual desire something against which struggle is imperative? Is it always and necessarily a desire comparable to the desire for many sexual partners or for sexual gratification at someone else's expense – comparable, more broadly to

the desire for revenge or the desire to avoid speaking an unwelcome or disadvantageous truth?[41]

To which, in part, the answer is that

'The phenomena of homosexual behaviour' are seen in a particular light in the Scripture – not as a uniquely awful perversion, but as an instance of the effect upon the human mind of rebellion against God, a symptom of that confusion that comes from failing to identify correctly and worship unreservedly the one true God.[42]

Thus, homosexual desire is not something in need of healing (and here Williams and John make slightly different points, because Dr John likens homosexuality to a disability which needs accommodating).

The question is about the basis on which a description of 'homosexual behaviour' and desire centred around Romans 1 can be given a privileged position over, let us say, a conscientious self-description by a homosexual person in terms of his or her longing to live a life in which their sexual desire, like other aspects of their identity, can come to image the love and the justice of Christ.[43]

So, Dr Williams could imagine a scenario where Christians with homosexual orientation would in good faith say that they do not recognize the condemnations of Romans 1 as describing them. They do not feel as though they are rejecting something they know to be part of their being. They do not want to live in promiscuity. They find it difficult to hear good news from the church if it insists that their homosexuality is 'spiritually compromised'.[44]

In order to address the problems of interpreting Romans 1, we need to decide upon what basis Paul makes the claim that something is 'natural' or 'unnatural'. Is it on the basis of the conduct of society members around him? If we are to understand anything of the crumbling Roman society and culture in which he wrote, then we must assume that he was greatly at odds with the 'natural' conduct of those around him. Two points need to be made.

First, here as elsewhere in his letters (1 Cor. 11), it is the departure from the created order that gives the evidence of God's judgement. What is natural is defined by creation, not by culture. In the context of the condemnation on idolatry and the denial of the knowledge of God, the implication is that perverted sex, whether heterosexual or homosexual, is creature-worship, rather than creator-honouring.

Gagnon notes the parallels in language between the LXX of the Genesis creation accounts and Romans 1. For example the words 'likeness', 'image', 'human', 'birds', 'four footed animals', and 'reptiles' occur in both Romans 1:23 and Genesis 1:26, making a striking point that Paul assumes that both idolatry and same-sex intercourse reject God's created order.[45]

It is not the innateness of the desires which dictates how we should behave: rather, according to Paul, it is the material creation and the bodily design of human beings. Otherwise Paul would be forced to list all the vices of 1:29-31 as 'against nature'.

> To suppose that Paul was condemning only the participation in homosexual acts by those who are 'naturally' attracted to the opposite sex 'is equivalent to saying that scriptural condemnation of adultery refer only to such relationships among those who are "naturally" monogamous'.[46]

Secondly, whether or not Paul recognizes a distinction between inversion and perversion is anachronistic. Paul's point is that the *conduct* is dishonouring to God — not because it goes against natural orientation.

Once again, Gagnon is helpful here. He makes the point that Paul picked up common Jewish rhetoric against homosexual acts (and the parallels with Wisdom 13 and elsewhere are very close), but he also appeals to the areas of Gentile agreement over homosexual and lesbian acts:

> Same sex intercourse is 'beyond' or 'in excess of' nature in the sense that it transgresses the boundaries for sexuality both established by God and transparent in nature even to the gentiles.[47]

> That Paul was thinking of 'nature' not as 'the way things are usually done' (i.e., cultural convention) but rather as 'the material shape of the created order' is also apparent from his previous illustration that idolatry entails the suppression of truth.[48]

Several sections of Gagnon's book are very helpful here, and in my mind, he makes the case very clearly: it is the misuse of what God has created, and not the passions and desires per se, that are against nature.

Two illustrations of this fact make the point.

From a purely biological point of view, human beings of the same sex are not made for intimate 'face-to-face' lovemaking, physically or genetically. Biology dictates that the vagina is made for the penis. The vagina has natural lubrication and multiple layers of protective skin cells in a way in which the anus does not; hence the dangers of infection and disease from anal sex are obvious. It is in this respect alone 'unnatural'. Secondly, as we noticed in Genesis 1 and 2, although procreation may not be the only goal of sexual intercourse, it is clearly a major part of it. Without heterosexual intercourse as the 'natural' expression of sexuality, the future of the human race would be in jeopardy.

Conduct Which Honours God?

The *Daily Mail* (Monday, 23 January 1995) printed an article by Mary Kenny entitled 'Gay Culture will never beat Nature', in which she interviewed lesbian couple Denise and Natalie Wilson, following the birth of baby Ellesse through artificial insemination. Whilst some applauded them for doing what comes naturally, Mary Kenny points out that their behaviour, 'far from being an affront to family values, ... is actually an inverted tribute to them ... the very idea of producing a child is intrinsically heterosexual'.

Clearly the 'nature versus nurture' debate continues, and it is not my intention to enter into the complexities of that argument.[49] All Christians believe that we are beings created in the image of God, but marred by the Fall. The effect of that Fall presumably has tainted both our nature (through inherited sin and its consequences) and nurture (through the fallen environment and sinful nature with which we live). It is not just learned sin for which the Bible assumes the need for repentance, but also original sin, the inherited sinful disposition (what the KJV translates as 'the flesh').

In a public statement in March 1995 the Bishop of London, the Right Revd David Hope (Now Archbishop of York), declared his own sexuality to be 'a grey area'. His statement has brought only partial comfort to Bible-believing Christians. It is encouraging that someone in his position has chosen to live a celibate life rather than disobey biblical teaching. It is discouraging, however, that even as a pastor of the flock he feels he cannot expect others to do the same. In his book *Evangelical Ethics,* John Davis has wisely commented that moral accountability is to be called for on the basis of conduct:

> Man brings a fallen human nature into a social environment that itself bears the marks of sin, and homosexuality is one of the distortions that can result from that interaction. The Bible has no illusions about the perfection of either human nature or the social environment, but it does hold man morally responsible for the way he interacts with his world.[50]

One final point on what constitutes 'sins against nature' concerns the expression of human sexuality. Martin Hallett has more to say about this in the interview. However, in the context of Romans 1:26f. the question arises: What is a *natural* (i.e., created and God-given) expression of sexuality? I think that it is important that we distinguish between what society dictates as sexual (or even gender) expression and what the Bible dictates as being against nature. I hope that we have clearly established the boundaries of conduct within God's created order. The question now arises over whether all expressions of sexuality are biblical/natural? For example, the Bible prohibits a woman from dressing in a man's clothes (see Deut. 22:5). But what exactly are man's clothes? Those to whom Paul was writing may well have worn clothes resembling contemporary women's dresses! Some church teaching today will still condemn a woman for wearing trousers.

Surely we must be sensible in interpreting this text? That which dictates *gender* expression is at least partly culturally defined. If a man wears a skirt and blouse he is making a counter-cultural statement. If a woman wears trousers she is not (necessarily). Deuteronomy 22 condemns transvestite and transsexual behaviour because it goes against nature. The way in which this deviant behaviour makes its expression varies according to the cultural expression of sexuality. It needs to be said that Christ-honouring conduct means being truly human — as we are created.

iii) Society suffers cultural and ethical disintegration (v.28ff.)

The breakdown of society is the third stage of the downward spiral following God's judgement upon sin. Any child nurtured in an environment where these sins are practised and where people 'invent ways of doing evil' is going to perpetuate the abolition of the foundations of the society as well as the destruction of the superstructure.

We have seen in our own country, the following trends:

a) Gender distinctions being abolished;
b) Gender roles are attacked;
c) Gender differences are denied.

The current issue related to homosexual conduct and its acceptance as normative falls into this third category. This breakdown reflects the cultural decline which would have been evident to Paul's readers.

From AD 68 onwards the Roman Empire was in a constant state of political and social upheaval. Here are two illustrations of the social and ethical degeneration which Paul could have witnessed around him, both showing how God had 'given them over' in their sin.

The first illustration of this can be evidenced in the social meeting place for Greek men at the *symposion,* social drinking and entertainment which took place in the 'men's room' (*andron*). The environment which the *symposion* provided was perceived as 'freedom' for the expression of sexuality outside family life. Women were never present at these social gatherings except as 'call girls'. However, the expression of emotions in a context free from the family setting was significant for the religious élite:

> Here is the main reason for the importance of homosexuality in ancient Greece; for the *symposion* provided the focus for liaisons of both 'earthly' and 'spiritual' type, whether in relation to fellow drinkers or the slave boys; the idealization of these emotions inspired some of the highest expressions of love in European literature.[51]

21

It is important to realise that the context of this homosexuality was an integration of 'religion' and 'culture'.

The second illustration may be seen in the life of the Emperor Nero. At the tender age of 17, Nero came to power in AD 54. His reign was marked by his obsession for the arts, increasing suspicion and sexual experiment. He committed suicide in AD 68 following threats from his political allies.

Sexual perversity was one mark of the Roman Emperors, but under Nero homosexuality became more openly tolerated. At slave sales, prettier boys would receive a higher price than other slaves, and castration and other 'tricks of the trade' were used to retain the youthful appearance of adolescents. Dio Chrysostom traces 'a sexual rogue's progress':

> Bored with harlots, he seduces well-bred girls and married women and when this too becomes tedious because it is too easy he turns in his last state of degeneracy to seducing boys.[52]

This 'sexual progression' (we prefer the word 'degression') is evidenced in Nero's marriage to Sporus, a man whom he dressed up as a woman, gave the name 'Sabina', and with whom he travelled as his married partner. After Nero's death, Sporus then married the prefect of the Praetorian Guard, Nymphidius Sabinus.[53] This latter illustration is particularly important because this open homosexuality was intertwined in the fabric of the social life, not just in a religious cultic setting. Some would have us believe that Paul was only dealing with homosexuality or adultery (πορνεια) in an idolatrous setting. Moreover, the 'mimicking' of marriage – a kind of covenanted same-sex love – was evident in Roman culture and would have been included under the condemnations of Romans 1:18ff.

Such cultural and social decline is being mirrored in the modern Western world. However, it is possible for the downward spiral to be reversed (see Rom. 12 :1ff.), so we turn to examine this process of redemption and reform.

3 Redemption

Martin Hallett, and many other Christian converts who have renounced homosexuality, talk about the fact that their *desires* have not totally changed since they became Christians, but they are being modified by the grace of God.[54] Their *behaviour* changed from the day they became Christians. Certainly there are Christians whose deviant sexual orientation has been overcome as a result of their conversion (that is, homosexual desire is removed from them), but this is not universal. For many the issue is one of obedience.

However, it needs to be recognized that I may have *heterosexual* desire which will lead me into sin if unrestrained — I am not free to exercise that in fornication (sex prior to marriage) nor in adultery (sex when one or other is already married to someone else). Philip Jensen stated in a conference address, to the initial surprise of the audience: 'I want you all to know that I am a non-practising adulterer.' In a typically blunt manner he woke up those who would like to think that they are 'safe' from sexual sins. If we have understood Jesus' Sermon on the Mount correctly, we should appreciate that the human heart is not incapable of any sin. God sees that behind actions are (controlled, or uncontrolled) desires. The issue of sexual orientation, though not unimportant, is not really relevant at this point. For I do not need to be engaged in sexual activity to be fully human, and abstinence and self-denial are more clearly hallmarks of the Kingdom than is free expression (see, for example, Matthew 19:12).

Let us first continue building our framework. What happens to those who are redeemed by the saving work of Jesus? We shall examine several biblical passages.

a) Free acceptance comes with an expectation of change

In this present debate, an evangelical doctrine has been in danger of misuse. I refer to the phrase: 'Love the sinner; hate the sin'. It is clear from Scripture that this adage is exemplified in the life of Jesus and his followers. We need to rehar Jesus' words to the woman caught in adultery (recorded in John 8). Both homosexuality and adultery are punishable by death in Leviticus 20:10, 13. The Pharisees were concerned that justice should immediately be meted out to the full extent allowable under the law, for this woman was caught in the very act of adultery. Jesus challenged them as to whether they had the right to implement this merciless punishment. Once her accusers had silently slipped away, Jesus turned to her and said: 'Neither do I condemn you'. We thank God for his free acceptance of even the worst of sinners. But these were not his final words to this woman. He also said: 'Go and sin no more' (John 8:11b, KJV; 'leave your life of sin', NIV).

Similar teaching is to be found in the writings of Paul. In Romans 8 Paul comes to a tremendous climactic statement concerning the free acceptance which is ours through the justifying work of Christ: 'There is now no condemnation for those who are in Christ Jesus' (v.1). But as Romans 8 progresses it becomes clear that our very acceptance includes with it an expectation of change, for only change is evidence that justification has happened. There is no condemnation for those who are in Christ Jesus, but there is a new 'obligation' — not to the sinful nature, but to put to death the misdeeds of the body (v.12f.).

I am concerned that *loving the sinner and hating the sin* has been retranslated into *loving the sinner by never condemning the sin*. Michael Vasey asks the question:

> Would the Jesus of the Gospels have had gay friends and have been at home in a gay bar? The answer to both questions must be Yes.[55]

If we asked the question: 'Would Jesus have been happy to meet sinners where they were?', the answer has to be Yes. (Indeed, if we were to ask the modern church whether we are happy to meet sinners where they are, the answer sadly is often No). However, we have falsely divorced the friendship of Jesus from his moral expectations. He is never happy to leave us where we are. In a similar way it has been mistakenly assumed that the moral absolutes of Leviticus 18 and 20 have been abolished in the fulfilment of the law. To deal with the whole of the law as if it all related to land-based, cultural provisions is to do a severe injustice to the abiding significance of the moral absolutes (see further below). The fact that the severe judgement of the law is not always meted out is not an indication that the law no longer applies but that mercy is offered. The whole issue raised by Vasey[56] of the place of the law in the formation of contemporary ethics needs much greater attention than these few sentences, but space does not provide the opportunity. Nor is it necessary to restate the excellent work done by others in identifying how the ancient law applies to the modern church/culture.[57]

Far from abolishing the law, Jesus indicated that its demands were much higher than the simplistic Pharisaic reductionism. The Sermon on the Mount is particularly pertinent in this debate. In Matthew 5: 27-30 Jesus indicates that the sin of adultery is much wider than the genital act. The lust which man entertains in his heart is on a continuum with the act. This does not mean that there is no difference between the two; one is certainly a greater sin than the other. Neither do Jesus' words mean that we are at liberty to judge people's hearts; that alone is God's prerogative. However, it does mean that mere abstinence from extramarital sexual acts (whether hetero- or homosexual) is not the only issue. A new attitude and desire needs to be cultivated whereby bad desires are starved and good desires are fed. A new lifestyle and culture needs to be built up in the place of the old. In other words, we are not at liberty to assume that Jesus will pour new wine into old wineskins. The new life must develop into a new lifestyle, which includes a new mind (Rom. 12:1), a new hunger for God's Word (1 Pet. 2:2), a new character (Rom. 5:4), and new desires (Heb. 13:18). We shall see in a moment that the change which is expected by Jesus is indeed revolutionary, and must ultimately result in the reform of the character and the culture — indeed, nothing less than the reversal of the downward spiral of Romans 1:24ff.

b) Disordered lives are adopted into a new family

Vasey is surely correct to challenge the church's traditional approach to (nuclear) family life. There is a danger that the current emphasis on family as the normal expression of Christian lifestyle does an injustice to the many in contemporary culture who are not in what is perceived to be 'normal family life'. Much of the modern approach to church family life has more to do with middle-class, fairly affluent and educated values than it does with the Bible. Indeed, as Vasey points out, the New Testament churches (see 1 Cor. 5; 1 Tim. 5) had a variety of social and domestic expressions within the church. However, I am not sure that Paul would recognize the conclusions which Vasey draws from this diversity:

> The various sexual and domestic arrangements envisaged in the Old Testament — with its acceptance of divorce, polygamy and considerable male sexual activity outside the home — are evidence that societies, and even the people of God, cannot avoid compromise. It is interesting to note the widespread accommodation that evangelical Christians have made with divorce, even among Christians ... a similar pastoral principle is operating: people's need for viable social arrangements and affirming personal and sexual relationships have to be taken into account. A distinction is being made between what compromise arrangement is to receive a measure of recognition in the community and what uncompromised standard the individual is invited to consider.[58]

Once again we would want to endorse the biblical view that the new Christian finds in the Christian community acceptance, love, new relationships, and maybe even a new and alternative family with our brothers and sisters in Christ. The gospel does not first call us to a new lifestyle in Christ without adopting us *into* a new family: with Christ as our brother and God as our Father — and a whole family of Christian relations. Within this community, as well as within the lives of the individuals who make it up, there will be evidences of man's fallen condition. This ongoing sinfulness needs to be repented of, and forgiveness sought from God. What the Bible does not assume will happen is that fallen behaviour will be integrated into the church as if it was normal and acceptable. This is, sadly, the very 'compromise' which is happening in the modern church.

The famous passages in 1 Corinthians 5:1-12 and 6:9-20 are written out of pastoral concern for the holiness of God's church. Paul clearly assumed that a radical new lifestyle would follow a change of heart. The Christian community in Corinth included those who *were* sexually immoral (πόρνοι — literally adultery, fornication — this word is also used symbolically throughout the LXX as a symbol of the departure from faithfulness to God, and Paul clearly has the former usage in mind). There were idolaters (εἰδωλολάτραι), adulterers (μοιχοὶ — refers to sexual relations outside of marriage), male prostitutes (μαλακοὶ — Gordon Fee points out that behind the NIV translation is a fuller meaning of this word, the basic meaning being 'soft', a contemporary word used by Philo for the effeminate, passive partner in a homosexual relationship[59]) and homosexual offenders (ἄρσενοκοῖται — which more than likely refers to the active, homosexual partner who engages in, literally, 'male intercourse'). We may summarize Paul's conclusion: 'Such were some of you, but you have changed as a result of the justifying and sanctifying work of the Holy Spirit' (cp. 1Cor. 6:11).

If it is true that homosexuality is the outcome of deficient same-sex relations in family life — an overbearing or absent father effecting the orientation of boys, or an absent or dysfunctional mother effecting the orientation of girls — then surely in the *family of God*, Christians with homosexual tendencies *should* find some compassion, relief from loneliness and isolation, and healthy same-sex friendships. John Stott quotes Dr David Atkinson:

> We are not at liberty to urge the Christian homosexual to celibacy and to a spreading of his relationships, unless support for the former and opportunities for the latter are available in genuine love. [60]

When we think about the impact redemption will have upon the homosexual, Vasey is surely correct to conclude his discussion by asking the question: 'What is homosexuality?' This is the crucial question. The answer must at least include the basic ethical prohibitions of the Bible. For this author at least, the area of debate concerns how we define lifestyle that is honouring to God in the light of the absolutes which are dictated. However, it does not seem to be the issue for Vasey, which returns us to our key issue concerning the sufficiency of Scripture in the debate. For example, the following questions which Vasey asks reveal more than maybe he intends about his attitude to the Bible:

> Did the Emperor Hadrian's much celebrated love for the handsome Antinous make him less than a real man? Did Richard the Lion Heart's sexual passion for Philip, king of France, make him effeminate? Do William of Orange's secret nights with a young captain make him a homosexual? Do more than a hundred sonnets addressed by Shakespeare to a young man make him gay? Such questions may serve to challenge common stereotypes about gay people. They also provide a useful introduction to the modern debate between essentialist and constructionalist understandings of homosexuality. Obviously men have sex with other men. The question being debated is whether there is such a thing as homosexuality — a psychological condition and social identity which transcends culture. [61]

It has to be said in the clearest possible way that *this is not the debate for evangelical Christians*. If there is any debate, it concerns how we are to define conduct that will honour God according to the clear prohibitions which exist in Scripture, which may include social and cultural rethinking about true friendships between people of the same sex.[62] To seek to redefine how we view homosexuality in the light of the prevalence of homosexual deviance in contemporary culture is to show that we do not believe that the Bible is authoritative and normative for our conduct.

4 Return

Our study has emphasized the fallen nature of the human condition. This, I believe, is right. We must be biblical realists if we are going to understand our behaviour from

God's perspective. We have noticed in the preceding section that, through the redeeming work of Jesus Christ, God does change lives. Part of the eschatological first-fruits enjoyed now, as a foretaste of heaven (Rom. 8:23) is that some will enjoy the healing of their homosexual orientation.[63]

However, it is also true that the homosexual and the heterosexual seeking to live in obedience to God will continue to groan inwardly, awaiting the perfect body which God has in store for us in the future. That work of recreation is not yet completed. In Romans 13:8ff. the motivation to live and think differently is the coming of the Day (of judgement), that is, the return of Christ. Love is the fulfilling of the law (v.10f.) which is expressed in behaving 'decently, as in the daytime, not in orgies and drunkenness, not in sexual immorality and debauchery, not in dissension and jealousy ... do not think about how to gratify the desires of the sinful nature'. It is the indwelling by God the Holy Spirit which causes the Christian to groan, waiting for the redemption of our bodies (Rom. 8:23), but also empowers the Christian to live differently (Rom. 8:9ff.).

The symbolism of sexual purity is frequently used in Revelation 17 onwards, implying not only that adultery and fornication will be eradicated, but that, so too, will homosexuality. Presumably the words of Jesus in Matthew 22:30 refer specifically to the fact that there will be no more need of procreation, and hence the absurd scenario of the Sadducees is irrelevant. The picture of ongoing, loving relationships in heaven is frequently used. All of this is no more than that which was promised by the prophets in the Old Testament — the free acceptance into God's kingdom by a gracious God, whatever may have previously been done, including the eunuch's physical changes (see Isa.56:33f.). The wonderful expectation of Ephesians 5:33 is that the fulfilment of Genesis 2:24 is found in the glorified church. The human marriage covenant, in the complementary union of male and female, is God's enacted parable of the end-time union between Christ and his bride (the church). Such an analogy clearly breaks down if there is an attempt to reverse the roles of husband and wife (for that, by analogy, would make Christ subservient to the church), or male and female complementarity is substituted by same-gender intimacy of this kind.

The pushmi-pullyu

Dr Dolittle's extraordinary character of this name with one body, four legs and two heads has fascinated children for generations.[64] However could such a creature move without tearing itself in two? The answer has to be that one head chooses to give way to the other. When the one takes the lead, the other consents to follow in order that progress may be made, and vice versa.

When we discuss what kind of behaviour is Christ-honouring, there is a pushmi-pullyu effect. The twin influences upon our behaviour are that of obedience (to God's stated will in the Bible) and love (as the fulfilling of the law). It is not Christ-honouring to put one over the other, nor to assume that one overrides the other. 'Remaining in the Son' comes about by obeying God's commandments, which in themselves may be summarized as the command to love (John 15:9-17). When John further amplifies Jesus' remarks in 2 John 5f., he makes it clear that whilst either love or obedience may lead the way, it is not one without the co-operation of the other.

From this, two simple deductions may be made concerning Christ-honouring conduct. First, love must be defined by obedience. Godly, loving behaviour is that which takes God at his word and chooses to obey irrespective of whether the feelings or desire to do so are dominant.

Secondly, obedience must be tempered by love. The Bible does not allow a place for blinkered legalism. Feelings of love and desire for God follow will-motivated obedience. God not only gives us his directives in his Word, but he also plants within us the desire to obey his Word out of love for Christ.

Christ-honouring conduct is nothing less than the changing of our whole being into Christ-likeness (will, desire, mind, and affections).

Where the battle rages most fiercely

Martin Luther said:

> If I profess with the loudest voice and clearest exposition every portion of the truth of God except precisely that little point that the world and the devil are at that moment attacking, I am not confessing Christ, however boldly I may be professing Christ. Where the battle rages fiercely is where the loyalty of the soldier is proved, and to be steady on all the battlefield besides is merely flight and disgrace if he flinches at that point.[65]

Since 1995, the area of conflict has surrounded the authorization of liturgies to bless same-sex unions in covenanted friendships. The File quoted above was written by Dr Packer in response to the decision, in June 2002, by the diocese of New Westminster to authorize a form of same-sex unions.

Dr Rowan Williams has written:

> There is now a fairly familiar suggestion that, if what is symbolically central in the scriptural view of marriage, in Old and New Testaments, is not an arrangement for procreation but a condition of living 'under promise', living in commitment *usque ad mortem* ... *crucis*, then the partnership of two persons of the same sex is in some way 'showing' what marriage shows of the God who promises and who remains faithful.

... a major goal in what I have written here is to enter a plea for some recognition of the fact that those who want to argue what I have called a revisionist position on the possible legitimacy of 'sexual expression' for the person of homosexual inclination may, like their opponents, be trying to find a way of being faithful and obedient to the givens of revelation.[66]

The argument goes: If it is established that homosexuality is something which is genetically or otherwise conditioned (an argument which, in fact, has by no means been conclusively settled), then homosexuality is either a gift of God, or a disability to live with — depending on whom you follow – which needs to be accommodated. Is it right that the church should condemn people with this natural orientation, to a life without sexual expression? Moreover, some people advocate that Romans 1 (and more particularly Genesis 19) speak of perverted behaviour and promiscuity as alien to the sensitive invert as to any heterosexual.

So, Dr Jeffrey John asks, having clearly established that non-procreative sex is acceptable among heterosexual Christians, what good reason is there to forbid it amongst homosexually orientated people? To be sure, the Scripture condemns promiscuous sex: thus, some kind of understanding of same-sex attraction — to include intimacy, companionship, friendship and sexual expression — should be recognized by the church.

> Of course for the majority of people heterosexual marriage is the ideal — and there are faithful married clergy to exemplify it. For those who are called to celibacy, faithful celibacy is the ideal, and there are faithful celibate clergy to exemplify that also, I have argued that for homosexuals who are not called to celibacy a faithful covenanted partnership is the ideal ...[67]

Commenting on the introduction to the marriage service, John says, 'Would we deny that means of fulfilment to two heterosexual people who wished for and were capable of it? Why then would it occur to us to deny it to two homosexual people?'[68]

> It seems to me inhumane and un-Christian (in a profound, not trivial sense) to deny that hope to so many men and women whom God has created for ultimate fulfilment – yes – but a fulfilment which will only be reached through our learning in this life to love one another in this way. That is why I believe we have an absolute duty in the Church to offer homosexual couples, clerical and lay, not merely a grudging admission, but a positive theological understanding of their relationship, just as we do heterosexual couples in marriage, to help them realise the same hope, the same ideal, of secure, faithful, lifelong love.[69]

The compassionate and eloquent argument of Dr John sounds compelling. Those of us who know him also realize that to label him as a gay rights activist in the way the press did in the summer of 2003 is just not fair. Jeffrey John is a thoughtful, committed person who sincerely believes under God that the model of covenanted faithfulness is the most appropriate way to express his love for his lifelong partner.

The problem with this argument, however, is that if the incontrovertible conclusions reached above indicate that same-sex sexual activity is contrary to God's will – irrespective of whether the participant is in a stable partnership, and irrespective of whether they are sexually-oriented that way – then to normalize and perpetuate this relationship, blessed by covenant, is wrong. Moreover, it would not just be wrong but it would be disastrous for the church. Thoughtful homosexuals talk about the pressures to be unfaithful, with multiple partners, being caused in part by the church's failure to recognize the givenness of their 'inversion'. I would want to say, however, that lapses in sexual conduct, whether heterosexual of homosexual (or bestial or incestuous), by the grace of God are forgivable for the penitent. The blessing of a same-sex union involves normalizing conduct which God has deemed 'against nature', and it is to allow persistent sinners to continue in their sin, without condemnation and with no call to repentance. Is this better than occasional lapses? I fear not!

True Union in the Body was commissioned by the Most Revd Drexel Wellington Gomez, Archbishop of the West Indies. Arguing, quite powerfully, that what we do with our bodies affects the body life of the church (p.4, cf. 1 Corinthians), this document gives a considered response to the call to bless same-sex unions.

> ... the decision to bless same-sex unions, rather than assisting a life of faithful witness and being good pastoral practice, sends out contradictory messages concerning the Christian life. It undermines the faithful witness by leading Christian believers into areas of real temptation and indeed sin. Faced with a confusing array of voices from the prevailing culture, many Christian people (especially young people) struggle in the formation of their self-understanding as sexual beings and in their desire to be faithful to the call of Christ. It is therefore imperative that the Church be seen to uphold clearly the divinely given norms to which true humanity aspires. [70]

This issue is very important. For Scripture makes it clear that what we do with our bodies affects both our personal spirituality and the body of Christ. In a perceptive article entitled 'Why this Issue?', Edith Humphrey has argued: 'Unlike Gnosticism, the Christian Way does not teach that what is done in the body is irrelevant, or that what is "spiritual" is more important than what is "physical".'[71] It is not possible to abuse the human body and assume that it does not affect your spirituality.

Similarly, false teaching and practice in the body of the church has very serious consequences for the world-wide communion. This is Wolfhart Pannenberg:

> Here lies the boundary of a Christian Church that knows itself to be bound by the authority of Scripture. Those who urge the church to change the norm of its teaching on this matter must know that they are promoting schism. If a church were to let itself be pushed to the point where it ceased to treat homosexual activity as a departure from

the biblical norm, and recognized homosexual unions as a personal partnership of love equivalent to marriage, such a church would stand no longer on biblical ground but against the unequivocal witness of Scripture. A Church that took this step would cease to be the one, holy, catholic, and apostolic church.[72]

The church must speak clearly

The church must speak clearly, and on this particular issue, which will put us most at odds with the prevailing culture around us. It is our duty to try to halt these downward moral trends, through prayer, speaking and action. Controversial American Bishop Jack Spong analyses six steps, or stages, of acceptance of homosexuality by churches:

a) The issue is discussed. This in itself is significant because 'one does not debate such self-evident evils as murder, rape, arson and child molesting'.

b) Homosexuals are declared God's children: 'hate the sin, love the sinner'.

c) Homosexuals' civil rights, when threatened by society, are defended by the church.

d) It is recognized that the homosexual orientation is not chosen and thus is not sinful. Consequently we stop fearing that our children will be 'made homosexual'.

e) It is recognized that the homosexual orientation is morally neutral, and the expectation of celibacy is removed.

f) The church explores how one leads a responsible sexual life as a homosexual.[73]

We must speak to the world around
- about their created potential in Christ;
- about the implications behind the presuppositions of their ethics;
- about their accountability before the judgement seat of God;
- about the redemptive and renewing work of Christ.

Francis Schaeffer's book, *Death in the City*, was first published in 1969, but his comments are just as relevant (if not more so) in the contemporary cultural scene. Commenting on the prophetic voice of Jeremiah to the foolish Jews in Jerusalem, he says:

> ... there is a time, and ours is such a time, when a negative message is needed before anything positive can begin. There must first be the message of judgement, the tearing down. There are times, and Jeremiah's day and ours are such times, when we cannot expect a constructive revolution if we begin by emphasizing the positive message. People often say to me, What would you do if you met a really modern man on a train and you had just an hour to talk to him about the gospel? I would spend forty-five or fifty minutes on the negative, to show him his real dilemma — to show him that he is

more dead than even he thinks he is; that he is not just dead in the twentieth-century meaning of dead (not having significance in this life) but that he is morally dead because he is separated from the God who exists. Then I would take ten or fifteen minutes to tell him the gospel.[74]

We must speak to the Christian Church
- with biblical teaching;
- to reduce fear and 'homophobia';
- to equip them to bring others to Christ;
- to call the Church to repent of unrepentant behaviour and unbiblical teaching;
- to help them to model Christ-likeness to the world around.

There is still much to be done in working out the implications of Michael Vasey's teaching, subsequently followed up by Rowan Williams and Jeffrey John. In the Appendix I have tried to list some of the most common 'popular' objections to the conclusions reached above.

However, I believe that these conclusions, whilst full of human error, still contain the perspicuity of the Scripture in them! I pray that you and God will forgive my errors. But I also pray that the voice of Scripture would be clearly heard and that his Word would be heeded and put into practice in his church. All too often it is the very clarity of Scripture which we find offensive. And, in this matter, I believe that to be the case. Evangelical Christians have been the target of slander and vitriol – both in the national press, and from outspoken liberals in the denomination. My hope is that this booklet will help 'steady our nerve' on this issue, and give us boldness to 'speak the truth in love' (Ephesians 4:15) and like our master, be full of both 'grace and truth' (John 1:14b).

Will I live to eat my words on this issue? Scripture, Tradition and Reason seem to indicate otherwise. For my part, I stand with Martin Luther at the Diet of Worms:

> Unless I am convinced by testimonies of the Scriptures or by clear arguments that I am in error – for popes and councils have often erred and contradicted themselves – I cannot withdraw, for I am subject to the Scriptures I have quoted; my conscience is captive to the Word of God. It is unsafe and dangerous to do anything against one's conscience. *Here I stand*; I cannot do otherwise. So help me God.[75]

Appendix

Sound-Bite Answers to Popular Objections

❖ **Jesus did not say anything about homosexuality, so why should we?**

It is very difficult to make substantive points from 'arguments from silence'. It is true that Jesus did not make direct reference to the subject of homosexuality. However, he upheld the holiness codes of Leviticus; he pointed to Genesis 2:24 as the created norm and expectation for life-long marital faithfulness; and he was born into a theological and social setting which almost universally condemned sexual activity outside marriage. Jesus condemns πορνεῖαι (Matthew 5:32; 15:19; 19:9), which includes sex outside marriage. For Jesus to have approved of homosexuality would have required him to have specifically overturned the clearly received teaching of the Old Testament. Moreover, if it was the case that the argument about homosexuality rests purely on Vasey's 7 knock-down texts[76] (which it doesn't), should the reader not be concerned that there is not one single statement in the Bible positively affirming same-sex sexual activity?

Jesus' silence on this matter should not be considered to be assent.

❖ **We know so much more about homosexuality today: the Bible is out of date and irrelevant.**

First, how much more do we know? There is evidence that, within Graeco-Roman culture, it was thought that some people existed with a natural attraction to those of the same sex.

Secondly, the condemnation of homosexuality is not based upon the cultural expectations at the time of writing the Bible: rather, it is based upon God's created intention for human beings (hence Romans 1:20, 26-28).

Thirdly, the complex discussion concerning the origins of homosexuality (whether it be by an overbearing or absent parent, or the unlikely discovery of the 'gay gene') are, in my view, not really relevant here. The Bible speaks about sinful human nature being both 'taught' and 'caught'. In other words, I sin *in* Adam and I sin *like* Adam. So Philip Jensen is right to say: 'I am a non-practising adulterer' because the issue here is obedience to God's clear commandments, not my natural propensity or desire for fulfilment.

❖ **If you wear poly-cotton shirts and eat prawns, how can you condemn homosexuality?**

John Richardson has recently answered this question more fully in his booklet *What God has made clean ...*[77].

Levitical texts condemn homosexuality, the eating of fish which do not have fins and scales (such as prawns) and black pudding! – and the wearing of garments made of mixed fabric (Leviticus 18:22; 20:13; 19:19; 19:26; 11:12).

The question poses a further one: Does homosexuality come into the catalogue of land-based Israelite laws concerning dress and food? Or does it come more clearly in the moral framework of the Ten Commandments? It is clear from the New Testament that Jesus declared all foods to be 'clean' (Mark 7:19), but Jesus did not do away with the law (on the contrary, Matthew 5:17-19). Moreover, Jesus clearly seems to place issues of sex in the category of *moral* law (Matthew 19:7-9).

❖ **Condemnation of homosexuality is unloving and intolerant.**

Here the church does need to hold up its hands and admit that we have been guilty of unloving attitudes towards homosexual people. Does our church look like Corinth – full of former prostitutes, former homosexuals, former swindlers, former drunkards – full of people who have been washed, sanctified and justified by the Lord Jesus? (see 1 Corinthians 6:9-11). Most of our churches are miles away from reaching these people with the gospel.

Secondly, though, we do need to reiterate Jesus' words to the woman caught in adultery (John 8) *'neither do I condemn you... go and sin no more'*. Jesus offered free forgiveness but also commanded departure from a life of sin. This is the loving thing to do!

Thirdly, it is important that we understand the biblical teaching on love and tolerance. For, as Gagnon points out,[78] they are not identical concepts. God *loves* the whole world, but does not tolerate sin! The church in Ephesus is actually commended for its *intolerance* of false teaching (Revelation 2:1-7). Thus a church which tolerated sexual immorality is not commended by Jesus, but rather it is castigated.

Finally, what is the most loving thing to do when someone is in impending danger? The most loving thing to do is to warn them and to rescue them. This is precisely what needs to happen in this debate. Though the issue may *feel* very personal for someone struggling with sexual temptation, the most loving and tolerant thing we can do is: 'Love the sinner and hate the sin'.

❖ The church is hung-up on the issue of sex, and speaks out too little about greed and pride.

A little earlier, I mentioned Edith Humphrey's perceptive comment about Gnosticism. What we do with our body matters deeply to our spirituality. The Gnostics believed that they could drag their bodies through sin, but their souls would be unharmed. They illustrated their point by dropping a pearl in mud, picking it up, and showing that once washed it remains undamaged. Sexual sin is not like that. We do harm to ourselves and our communities.

The point at issue here concerns the approval of sins which the Bible has expressly condemned (Romans 1:32). To my knowledge there are not too many Christian churches arguing that greed, in fact, is not a sin, but a virtue, and that pride and arrogance are human qualities we should commend and celebrate. The reason why this issue is so important in the Anglican denomination at the moment is that there are Christian leaders who are seeking to further, and approve, a view of same-sex relations which the majority of Christians across the world, and the majority of Christians down the ages, believe to be against Scripture. For both of these reasons, whilst we need to be careful about selecting *other people's sins* for condemnation (and not our own), this issue of sex is of major concern to the health of the Christian and the body of Christ.

❖ If love is the fulfilling of the law, who are you to judge another person's behaviour?

Like the pushmi-pullyu, both heads need to defer to each other in order not to rupture the body!

Love is the fulfilling of the law (Romans 13:10), but to live the life of love includes not engaging in orgies, sexual immorality and sensuality, nor gratifying the desires of the flesh (v13). Love involves walking according to God's commandments (2 John 6) but the prime commandment is that of love. Love requires me to express love towards others, but law dictates the appropriate ways in which that love is to be manifested.

It is not my business to judge another person's heart (although Jesus will do so, according to Matthew 5:21ff.). However, it is right that the church comments on, and commends, certain types of behaviour which are appropriate.

❖ It is increasingly being concluded that homosexuality is innate and unchangeable. Is it wrong to offer 'inverts' celibacy as the only pathway to sexual holiness?

Here I do wonder whether, in our oversexed society, we have mistakenly assumed that a person is unfulfilled if they are unable to have sex. It is unhelpful that David's relationship with Jonathan, and Jesus' relationship with the beloved disciple, have been besmirched by the view that they may have been sexually active.[79] It is wrong to assume that all desire is good and godly. The most common New Testament word for desire is ἐπιθυμία, which is a neutral word. The rightness or wrongness of the desire in question is determined by whether the desire is Godward and honouring, or self-ward and dishonouring. C.S. Lewis wrote a famous book entitled *The Four Loves*.[80] True fulfilment is not found in *eros* alone. The other three loves are essential for fulfilment and healthy relationships in the church. As Christian communities, we do need to *love one another and serve one another*, but not in ways that indulge the sinful nature (Galatians 5:13).

> ❖ **The church's interpretation of key texts about women and slaves has proved to be wrong. Will we not subsequently find this to be the case with the issue of same-sex relationships?**

There is a very modern danger, and that is the assumption that the modern church is more likely to be right than the ancient church.

I would also want to ask: Have we got the issue of male/female relationships more correct now than we had prior to the rise of Feminism? Repenting of past chauvinism and male arrogance is, and was, very important. But throwing out the bathwater of male/female inequality and the baby of male/female complementarity has not helped us very much! At some point in the discussions of the last 30-40 years we have moved from a healthy desire to treat women with full equality, to the modern scenario where all gender distinctions have been dissolved.

Slavery is another case in point. In the New Testament, the treatment expected of slaves was quite radical and counter-cultural to the day (see Philemon, for example). Moreover, some of the cultural understanding related to slaves more along the lines of employees, than as servants. Texts such as the much quoted (and much misunderstood) Galatians 3:28, affirms the complete equality of all people in Christ. And, yes, the church under Wilberforce and others was right to see the incongruity of the buying and selling of human beings for slavery and the freedom which the gospel offers human beings.

The current discussions about same-sex relationships have moral implications which take us back to God's creative intentions for men and women, and it seems to me that there are issues here which transcend modern and current social and cultural concerns.

An interview between Simon Vibert and Martin Hallett of the True Freedom Trust

1) Can you define homosexual behaviour?

I see that there are lots of ways in which we express our sexuality, not just in terms of having an orgasm with someone. I think we are expressing our sexuality in all our relationships, whether we are attracted to someone or not. Even if it is a negative expression, it is nevertheless an expression of our sexuality. Therefore, because I am aware of homosexual feelings, I am expressing those when I relate to a number of people. The key issue is the way in which I am expressing those feelings — are they legitimate as far as God is concerned? I would say that the genital expression of those feelings is not legitimate, but Jesus also clearly condemns certain attitudes of mind as well as physical acts. This attitude applies heterosexually as well. Sexuality needs to be seen in a wider context than just orgasm. This means that I do not cease to be a sexual person if I am not involved in a genital sexual relationship.

2) I was brought up in a church environment where there was discussion about 'how far would be too far' with your girlfriend. Within the Christian church the debate has focused upon the act of sexual intercourse. Hence the taboos concerning sex outside marriage have related to the debatable acceptability of a series of prior points before intercourse takes place.
a) How do you understand this debate to relate to acceptable homosexual or heterosexual conduct?

Again I would say that the debate has focused upon the sexual act. Something that is designed to lead a person to orgasm is obvious unhelpful. However, I think that we sometimes get the three words 'sexuality', 'sensual' and 'sex' confused. I was struck by a comment Elaine Storkey made in a lecture at Christian Impact in which she described Mary Magdalene's washing of Jesus' feet with her tears as a sexual and sensual act. Here was a prostitute doing something which was clearly interpreted as being very provocative in the eyes of the watching Pharisees. Yet Jesus affirmed her in what she did out of love for him. Our emotions are tied up with our sexuality, and in this way we relate to people on a much wider level than may at first be simplistically assumed.

b) Can you define those words: sex, sensual and sexuality?
What they mean to me may not be what they mean to someone else — the definition is affected by how I see it.

Sex involves genital contact with someone — seeking to arouse and please sexually, and may well lead to orgasm by either or both partners.

Sensual describes the way in which a person expresses his/her sexuality of masculinity or femininity in a manner which could be provocative and seeks to arouse and please a person sexually. It could be a 'come on' but it might not be — seeking a response, which may be done quite innocently.

This does have moral implications because one has to be sensitive to the way messages are portrayed, i.e. a girl walking down the street with a very short skirt. If she is doing this to try to turn people on, or be affirmed by people, that is not a good expression of sexuality. Indeed it is a bad one.

Sexuality expresses our gender distinctiveness. It does not mean that we are seeking a sexual response — it is our sense of being. Our sexuality is related to our being. Our emotions and our sexuality are interlinked, because they are a reflection of how we feel about ourselves and other people. They are not separate. A married man is expressing his heterosexuality within his marriage. But he does not therefore assume that he is denying his sexuality when relating to people in general.

It is often assumed that if one is celibate, one is having to deny his or her sexuality. I do not think so. It simply means that one is being faithful to the Lord sexually rather than simply to a spouse. The same applies to a married person in this respect.

The church has reflected sociological attitudes to sexuality. Society sees fulfilment as being tied up with sexual fulfilment. The church says that this is not true but, generally speaking, assumes that fulfilment is only found within the marriage setting.

3) Still considering the question of what behaviour is honouring to God, what are some of the implications regarding behaviour for someone coming from a background of practising homosexuality trying to reorientate into a Christian lifestyle?
As far as I was concerned, I have come to realize that mine was an unusual situation. Initially I was not struggling with sexual temptation, but I was aware of emotional feelings which I thought were okay provided they were expressed in God-honouring ways. So I could therefore start relating to people of the same sex in loving ways which were coming into line with the biblical definition of love. In other words, I did not need to seek a return of my love.

In the same context, when I later became aware of sexual temptations and feelings in some relationships as a Christian, I knew that they would actually harm the relationship. The things which I thought had been finally buried began to come to the surface in a particular situation. My incentive was now to make sure I walked down the right road, based upon my love and value for the other person. I also recognized that I was sometimes tempted to use sex to affirm me in a relationship, because I had been accustomed to being affirmed sexually. If I was wanted sexually, I was wanted, and therefore accepted. Therefore it was a temptation to know that I was pleasing to the other person sexually.

The other person enabled me to work through this by helping me to see that I was valued for who I was. This was of course a long process, but ultimately I came to believe that I was loved and loveable without having to think that I needed to be pleasing sexually.

4) Is there any difference in the kind of temptations and struggles experienced by any person coming to Christ, homosexual or heterosexual?

No, I do not think that there is. We are often tempted to think that there is, but this relates to issues of social acceptability. Ultimately there should be recognition that there is not any difference, because we are all sexual people.

5) I think that there is a credibility gap between what we may agree upon as we sit down and discuss theology and ethics, and the kind of reaction given in church circles. Why do you think that this is the case?

Because church people are also sexual people, there is no doubt that discussions like this bring very strong emotions to the surface and some of those emotions are based upon fear. When I talk to church groups, I often say that the people who shout out most strongly against homosexuality are people who are secretly struggling in that area. When you say that, you don't get a murmur out of people! Often, Christians who are struggling with sexual issues will come down with a heavy hand against those they perceive to be more deviant. This is what the psychologists call 'transference'.

On the other hand, because sex is such a strong driving-force (it is used to sell nearly everything these days) people will always respond when the issue is discussed. The media uses sex in subtle ways, playing upon our emotional reactions. Writing the words 'Baked Beans' on a piece of paper has little effect upon people. Write the word 'Sex' and you will arouse strong emotions. Hence, discussing sex and sexuality makes us more vulnerable than sometimes we realize. It is bound to bring strong feelings to the surface.

Because we do not talk about the issue of sexuality openly enough, the enemy more often has a heyday. The accuser will thrive on any area of secrecy. He will take advantage of it. I find that the biggest area of enemy condemnation is accusation.

6) What kind of sexual behaviour is honouring to God? What does the Bible expect of us?

It is behaviour that is helping the other person, as well as oneself, to honour God. Therefore it is not selfish or self-indulgent. Affection that is not seeking to arouse another person, or do the same to oneself, is likely to be honouring to God.

It is hard to be dogmatic, because so much of this involves what goes on in a person's mind. We need to be honest with ourselves about what is going on. Yes, set clear boundaries, but recognize that sometimes those boundaries may be a bit blurred.

We need to recognize the basic human need for love: to love and to be loved. Our definition of love should be one which is honouring to God (e.g.1 Cor.13). Yes, this is idealistic, but it is what we should be working towards. Therefore, if I am relating to someone whom I know is aroused sexually by my closeness then, even if I am not aroused myself, that is not loving them. Honesty and communication are important in any relationship — with oneself and with the other person.

Where there is this honesty, it is possible to respond when the desire for affirmation is couched in sexual terms by showing legitimate expressions of love to them. I have a friend who once said to me: 'Martin, don't spoil something which is beautiful'. By doing this he affirmed our relationship in a positive way, but equally said that, if I was walking down that relationship in a sexual way, even if he was not responding, it was spoiling the friendship. I use this as an illustration of how this helped me not to walk down a road which I know is not open to me. In such a situation the expressing of my sexuality in that way could have gone wrong.

7) Do you believe that celibacy is a calling? 'The only way to fulfilment is to be married' is what is tacitly assumed in church and, therefore, if the right person has not come along by default, I feel that I am called to celibacy.
I am called to be obedient to Christ and to be fully human, expressing that humanity in lots of different ways. I do not feel that I am celibate in the sense of incredible self-denial and deprivation, although in essence I must be. The 'eunuch for the Lord's sake' refers to all three types of people in Matthew 19: only the third had positively chosen that option. Perhaps I should say 'I feel called to be unmarried' as a better way of putting it.

8) At the risk of over-generalizing, it seems that a man is much more visually stimulated, whereas a woman tends to be more stimulated by emotional involvement. Therefore:
a) When we talk about arousal, do we have to deal with both of those issues?
As you know another person and are communicating honestly, intimacy can grow. When you are doing that, what stimulates someone will become apparent. Once we have that information we can abuse it or we can let it be honouring to God. If I know what somebody's vulnerabilities are, I can abuse that — which would not be loving. Equally, it could make me sensitive.

So, if I know that a person to whom I am relating is aroused by the touching of a leg, for example, then, if I am indifferent to that, I am not honouring God. What arouses comes from knowing another person.

b) Are there no objective criteria with which you would like to work? Surely I will arouse people with whom I have no relationship if I do not keep to certain boundaries of dress and behaviour attitudes?
I do not relate to everybody in the same way. If I am in a relationship with someone I know well, then sharing of affection and deeper intimacy may be appropriate. The way in which this works out becomes instinctive, but not legalistic. It is a question of being aware of one's self and of other people, and being sensitive to how they are reacting.

Abuse of trust need not be just a sexual thing. To pray in church too intimately for a lady with breast cancer may also come into that category.

. A handshake in Western culture is a customary greeting. To be offended by my shaking your hand would indicate that you are operating in a different cultural framework from me. The point is that the cultural expression will dictate what is or is not a sensual act.

9) In what way may the church better act as a community, an extended family, as a caring body? There are two reasons for asking this question:
a) What does it mean to be a church 'family'?
b) Is there a problem in the way which we emphasize the nuclear family in the church (family services, etc.)?
We do need to learn how to relate to one another in church and build upon the quality of those relationships, understanding legitimate human needs for security, for love, for closeness, for intimacy. These are needs which God has created within us and which can only be fulfilled in relating to another human being. Traditionally the church has assumed that it will only be possible to meet those needs within a marriage relationship. Yes, sexual intimacy is only for that context. But there are other areas of intimacy which are basic needs to be met within relationships in the church, both for married and unmarried. There is no blueprint, because each person is different. There are key issues, like commitment. Relationships which are based on a solid commitment before the Lord (e.g. Ruth and Naomi, David and Jonathan) are those in which you actually say before the Lord: 'I commit myself to a working relationship with this person'. That means you may be related to as a 'couple'. You have the security of knowing that you are in a relationship and are recognized as 'best/good friends'. Counselling of relationships in the church generally is only undertaken in the context of marriage or potential marriage. I have seen relationships of the kind I mention counselled together, which I think is important for building on the security of that friendship.

To take another example. When a single person is relating to a married person, they cannot relate in isolation, even though the unmarried person may be closer to one marriage partner than to the other, because the partner is to be seen as a whole and not a single person. Hence you love the marriage and the family as well as the partner. You always have to put the marriage of that person first. This may mean seeking to let the loved one go.

If we had these kinds of relationship within the church, a lot of teaching would be needed about how we relate to one another. But there would be a lot less loneliness, and there would be better marriages as well, because people would be taught how to relate to each other. A lot of Christian marriages fail because people are not used to relating to each other.

I find that in some of my closest relationships, if I have been possessive or demanding, it has been helpful to be relating to someone who has been concerned that I let go of the relationship in a positive way. The insecurity which I feel has been dealt with by their showing me that I am loved.

10) *How do we cope with feelings of loneliness?*

First, it is more than a physical and emotional thing. There is also a spiritual dimension to loneliness. Anybody who lives the Christian life will at times be lonely. That is why it is important that we learn to be alone with God. Henri Nouwen, in *Reaching Out*[81] says that we need to move from loneliness to aloneness with God. And then from aloneness with God to community. This means that I will value aloneness and treasure it as a special thing between me and God, me and myself, and me and another person, because it is creative and productive. That is different from loneliness. When I can do that I am likely to be less lonely. Although I have been lonely at times, I have never felt totally abandoned by God.

Secondly, I do quite a lot of speaking on the subject of 'Singleness' and at times I feel a bit of a hypocrite because I do not feel like a single person! That is not because I have 'heavy', in-depth relationships, but it is because there are people in my life who are special to me and for whom I am special. The sense of commitment in those relationships makes me feel that I am not alone.

Many Christians still fear the thought of loneliness in old age; they fear that they do not fit in; they feel that they are not being true to themselves. But the reality is that we are not alone and God is involved in everything which is going on. Amongst Christian people there is sometimes a split between what I feel about myself and my 'spirituality'. I think that we need to acknowledge our feelings, even when we may think they are not right, because to keep them in a separate compartment implies that God is not involved in them.

11) How do we stop being judgemental whilst preserving definite moral convictions?

We talk about 'loving the sinner and hating the sin'. Our definition of loving the sinner needs to be unwrapped, because loving the sinner means understanding him or her; it means appreciating the value of that person being made in the image of God, and seeing the value that person has to God. This will often mean affirming the rights and choices which that person has. In terms of homosexuality, Christians need to stand against prejudice, and stand for positive rights. Seeking to love and understand a person must come through communication.

I have seen this happen with those caring for AIDS sufferers. Discovering homosexuals as people rather than as sinners has enabled the Christian carers to like and love them and receive back love from them. Sometimes the quality of relationship which they are finding with these victims has forced them to rethink their theology, which concerns me a bit! But there is a positive side to that, which is the means this gives to help them love the sinner. The more I love a person, the less I want that person to be separated from God. Anything that causes that person's relationship with God to go amiss distresses me. I think that this is what loving the sinner/hating the sin must be. We need to appreciate that people from a homosexual background find it difficult to differentiate between their sexual behaviour and their personhood. Their identity is wrapped up in what they are doing. So whatever you may say to them theologically will still be perceived as hating the sin and the sinner — which is why we have to do all we can to break through that.

We must communicate truth by getting to know and understand a person. At times this means that if I am afraid the person to whom I am talking may react adversely, then I will say so. I will try to explain that, because I love them and care for them, I am acting in a certain way, or will not act in a certain way.

12) Is it true to say that there is an integrated lifestyle for a homosexual which needs to be completely worked through?

In some cases 'yes', but many homosexuals do have 'gay' and 'straight' friends and lead 'normal' lives. The people who are on the gay disco and club scene do not represent the total number of gays.

13) Is there not an awareness among homosexuals which produces a group identity, and even today, a 'counter-culture' feel?

That is so true. I found that, when I became a Christian, I could see the parallels between being gay and being a Christian. I would be with people and would say: 'I wonder whether so and so is a Christian?' I can see the similarities. Take language, for example. At one time the gay language was just for the gay subculture, so that they could communicate with each other and nobody else would know what they were talking about — even the word 'gay' illustrates the point.

We Christians cling to a Christian identity in very much the same way that gays cling to their identity. It is right and biblical that Christians primarily relate to other Christians. (Certainly there is much that is part of the Christian identity which is cultural rather than biblical, but we must not lose sight of the fact that the identity of a Christian is found in a Christian culture.)

The main reason for using a label is self-security. Part of the formation of a homosexual sexuality is a low self-image; hence the label will be used to give the homosexual security in their identity. It is more than just an ideology.

14) Since you have become a Christian, have there been any changes in your sexual orientation? In other words, are you now more aware of desire towards members of the opposite sex?
I am sure that I have moved on a continuum, but I have to say that I have never actually felt that I wanted to have heterosexual feelings. That could be a blind spot in me, but I have never had them. It may be because I have never felt I wanted to be married and have children. I am not necessarily convinced that God wants every person to have heterosexual feelings, in the sense that we understand heterosexual feelings. This could be what Matthew 19:12 is referring to. I would hope that I am open enough to being married. I can say that I relate to women in a different way now, but it is hard to know how much of that is sociological and how much is the result of being a Christian. Some homosexual men relate better to women than they do to men. That has not been my experience because I have always been brought up in a male environment. I first came face to face with women after I ran away from my all-male school and ended up in a secondary modern school at 14! I found it hard to relate to women; I did not know what to do. Since I have become a Christian I have related much more healthily with women, I think. Although I am still aware of homosexual feelings at times — there are occasions when my homosexuality could still be an issue for me in terms of strong temptation — God continues to deal with this in me.

The True Freedom Trust was founded in 1977 by Martin Hallett and Canon Roy Barker. Martin was involved in a homosexual lifestyle for over nine years before Jesus Christ dramatically changed his life in 1972. In 1984 TFT helped to set up a similar ministry in London known as Turnabout. Chris Metcalf (Turnabout's director) also knew a personal struggle with homosexuality before experiencing the life-changing power of the Lord Jesus Christ. In 1991 TFT and Turnabout merged. TFT now has staff of several full and part-time workers and volunteers.

Further information about the work of the True Freedom Trust may be obtained from:
The True Freedom Trust, PO Box 3, Upton, Wirral, Merseyside, L49 6NY
(Tel. 0151 653 0773) or PO Box 592, London SE4 1EF (Tel. 0208 314 5735).

Notes

[1] M.Vasey, *Strangers and Friends* (London: Hodder and Stoughton, 1995).

[2] T.Bradshaw (ed.), *The Way Forward?* (London: Hodder and Stoughton, 1997; revised edn, London: SCM, 2003).

[3] R.Williams, 'The Body's Grace' in *Theology and Sexuality: Classic and Contemporary Readings* (Oxford: Blackwell, 1989).

[4] See http://www.anglican-mainstream.net . Dr John withdrew his acceptance of this offer in July 2003.

[5] R.Gagnon, *The Bible and Homosexual Practice: Texts and Hermeneutics.* (Nashville: Abingdon Press, 2001).

[6] For example, the enthronement of Michael Turnbull as Bishop of Durham in 1994; the debate in the 'naming' of eighteen homosexual bishops by Outrage! at General Synod; the subsequent statement by the Bishop of London (now Archbishop of York), the Right Revd David Hope, that his sexuality was a 'grey area' but that he had chosen to lead a celibate life; the Primates Pastoral Letter following the Right Revd Roy Williamson's comments on BBC Radio 4 in which he implied that he would be happy to ordain a practising homosexual involved in a 'stable' relationship.

[7] *The Church of England Newspaper,* 10th June 1994.

[8] M.Vasey, *Evangelical Christians and Gay Rights* (Nottingham: Grove Ethical Studies No. 80, 1991), p.5.

[9] One wonders whether, using the same logic, it is my responsibility to read *Playboy* before I can speak clearly about lust or adultery?

[10] J.R.W.Stott, *The Contemporary Christian* (Leicester: IVP, 1992), p.13.

[11] ibid., pp.101ff.

[12] Vasey, *Evangelical Christians and Gay Rights,* p.5.

[13] Vasey, *Strangers and Friends,* pp.113ff.

[14] ibid., p.115.

15 As illustrated in the CEN letter quoted on p.8. See also, below, the controversial treatment of Genesis 19.

16 A position Dr Williams has posited several times to the media (e.g. BBC2 programme 'An Archbishop Like This', December 2002).

17 A.C.Thiselton, *The Two Horizons* (Exeter: Paternoster Press, 1980).

18 ibid., p.11.

19 D.F.Wells, *God in the Wasteland: The Reality of Truth in a World of Fading Dreams* (Leicester: IVP, 1994), p.106.

20 O.Guinness & J.Steel, *No God But God: Breaking with the Idols of Our Age* (Chicago : Moody Press, 1992), p.197.

21 Vasey, *Strangers and Friends*, pp.124ff.

22 For example, I have found B.G.Webb (ed.), *Theological and Pastoral Responses to Homosexuality*, Explorations 8 (Sydney: Open Book Publishers, Moore College,1994), very helpful. Also, essential reading now is R. Gagnon, op. cit.

23 See further L. Morris, *The Epistle to the Romans* (Leicester: IVP, 1988), p.33f; J.R.W.Stott, *The Message of Romans* (Leicester: IVP, 1994), pp.6f.

24 T.F.Torrance, *The Hermeneutics of John Calvin* (Edinburgh: Scottish Academic Press, 1988), p.62.

25 J.Calvin, *Introduction to the Epistles to the Romans: The Argument*, H.Beveridge (tr.), Calvin's Commentaries Vol. XIX (Grand Rapids, Michigan: Baker Book House, 1989 reprint), p.XXIX.

26 Torrance, loc. cit.

27 J.Calvin, *Institutes of the Christian Religion*, Vols I & II, (tr.), F.L.Battles, (Philadelphia: Westminster Press, 1960).

28 This is a big issue. J.Hurley, *Man & Woman in Biblical Perspective* (Leicester: IVP, 1981), affirms the centrality of marriage and importance of having children, but also argues that the context of family life is much broader than our 'nuclear family'. Rather, the Israelite household was as broad as the clan

and the tribe. Therefore, though they were exceptional, there was included in this domestic structure the place for the single and the widow (pp.21, 42ff.).

Two other Old Testament references are worth mentioning. In Genesis 38 the Levirate marriage is given as a provision for ongoing care of a wife after the failure of the husband to take the correct lead in the relationship. Secondly, the famous passage extolling the wife of noble character in Proverbs 32 shows that, though clearly her family comes first, the role she fulfils extends to trading in the marketplace and teaching. In other words, her role can not be narrowly defined as child-bearing alone.

[29] We shall observe in our treatment of Romans 1 that homosexuality is a further deleterious step beyond perverted heterosexual sex.

[30] D.S.Bailey, *Homosexuality and the Western Christian Tradition* (London: Longmans, 1955).

[31] D.Field, *The Homosexual Way: A Christian Option* (Nottingham: Grove Ethical Studies No. 9, 1980), p.10.

[32] 'Detestable' (NIV), 'abomination' (KJV), βδέλυγμα (LXX) can be used to refer to either a religious or moral offence. However, making this distinction does not necessitate that the activity which causes offence is only tied up with religious ritual. The abomination of idolatry is not just that the worshipper fails to honour the Jewish God: rather, idolatry (and these sexual sins) are anti-God — they go against God's created order by placing something in the way of the true honour of God. In other words, what is detestable about a man lying with another man is that it is *unnatural* (a word which also becomes key to the interpretation of Romans 1).

[33] Meaning 'to hold down, to stifle, to suppress'.

[34] This word comes from a root-word meaning 'to roam', and can mean 'error' (as in 1 Thess. 2:3), 'rebellion' (Jude 11), 'deception' (Eph. 4:14) or, here, 'perversion'.

[35] Vasey, *Evangelical Christians and Gay Rights*, p.13.

[36] ibid., loc. cit.

[37] ibid., p.14.

38 See A.Shead, 'Homosexuality and the church: historical survey', in B.G.Webb (ed.), op. cit., p.25.

39 *The Way Forward?*, p.50.

40 ibid., loc. cit.

41 ibid., p.14.

42 ibid., p.15.

43 ibid., p.17.

44 ibid., loc. cit.

45 Gagnon, op. cit., p. 290f.

46 ibid., p.391, referring to L.Boughton, 'Biblical Texts and Homosexuality: A response to John Boswell' (ITQ 58, 1992), pp.142f.

47 ibid., pp.389f.

48 ibid., pp.256f.

49 Many studies quote the famous research by Alfred Kinsey *(Sexual Behaviour in the Human Male [1948]* and *Sexual Behaviour in the Human Female [1953])* about the number of people with homosexual orientation and the belief that this was a common and natural lifestyle, although the conclusions reached are thought by many to be overstated. See J.R.W.Stott, *Issues Facing Christians Today* (revised edn), (London: Marshall Pickering, 1990), p.336f; Field, op. cit., pp.3f.

50 J.J.Davis, *Evangelical Ethics* (Philipsburg, New Jersey: Presbyterian and Reformed Publishing Company, 1985), p.111.

51 J.Boardman, J.Griffin, O.Murray, *Greece and the Hellenistic World* (Oxford History of the Classics), (Oxford: OUP, 1988), p.219.

52 Quoted by J.P.V.D.Balsdon in *Romans and Aliens* (London: Duckworth Press, 1979), p.226.

53 ibid., pp.229f.

[54] See M.Hallett, *Out of the Blue: Homosexuality and the Family* (London: Hodder and Stoughton, 1996); also C. Keane (ed.), *What Some of You Were* (Australia: Matthias Media, 2001).

[55] Vasey, *Evangelical Christians and Gay Rights*, p.7.

[56] Vasey, *Strangers and Friends*, pp.113ff.; pp.138ff.

[57] See D.Field, *The Bible and Christian Living* (London: Scripture Union, 1987), ch.4.

[58] Vasey, *Evangelical Christians and Gay Rights*, pp.12f.

[59] G.Fee, *The First Epistle to the Corinthians* (Grand Rapids, Michigan: W.B.Eerdmans, 1991), pp.243f.

[60] Stott, *Issues Facing Christians Today* (London: Marshall Pickering, 1990), p.360.

[61] Vasey, *Evangelical Christians and Gay Rights*, p.17.

[62] Martin Hallett's answers to this question are very helpful.

[63] *Pursuing Sexual Wholeness* (Tunbridge Wells: Monarch, 1990) is the story of one man, Andrew Comiskey, who testifies to healing from a homosexual lifestyle and orientation.

From a different perspective, an article by E. and L. Patterson in *The American Journal of Psychiatry*, December 1993, recounts the change in behaviour and subsequent orientation of eleven exclusively homosexual men, following their loving acceptance into a Pentecostal church and subsequent conversions. Changes occurred in their desires when stable same-sex and opposite-sex friendships were built. Seven are now happily married; four state that they wish to be married.

[64] H. Lofting, *The Story of Doctor Dolittle* (London: Penguin 1922, reprinted 1967).

[65] Quoted in J.I.Packer, *A 'No' to Same-Sex Unions'* (FWS File 5, 2003), p.12.

[66] *The Way Forward?*, pp.18f.

67   ibid., op. cit., p.55.

68   ibid., op. cit., p.58.

69   ibid., loc. cit.

70   *True Union in the Body?* (Oxford: Future of Anglicanism, 2002), 5:16, p.36.

71   July 2003. http://www.acinw.org/articles/DrEdithHumphrey.html

72   Quoted in *True Union in the Body*, p.45.

73   Quoted by A.Shead, op. cit., p.20.

74   F.A.Schaeffer, *Death in the City* (London: IVP, 1972), pp.60f.

75   Quoted in *A 'No' to Same-Sex Unions*, p.11.

76   Vasey, *Strangers and Friends*, pp.124ff.

77   John Richardson, *What God Has Made Clean ...* (New Malden: The Good Book Company, 2003).

78   Gagnon, op. cit., p.27.

79   Vasey, *Strangers and Friends*, p.235.

80   C.S.Lewis, *The Four Loves* (London: Fount, 1998).

81   H.Nouwen, *Reaching Out: The Three Movements of the Spiritual Life* (New York: Image Books, Doubleday, 1975).

ORTHOS

Other titles already published by Fellowship of Word and Spirit

11 Recovering the Word
The need for expository preaching today
James Philip

12 The Church in the Age of the TV Image
Dare we still preach?
Simon Vibert

13 The Baxter Model
Guidelines for pastoring today
Wallace Benn

14 Conduct which Honours God?
The question of homosexuality
Simon Vibert
o.p. now revised as Orthos 20

15 Evangelicals and the Word of God
Paul-André Dubois

16 Prophecy and Preaching
Acts and the church today
David Peterson

17 New Initiatives in Christian Initiation
Simon Vibert

18 Reforming the Denomination
Wallace Benn, Michael Lawson, Simon Vibert

19 By Word and Spirit
Two Archbishops on the Doctrine of Revelation
Simon Vibert

* Reprinted together under the title *The Church's Ministry*

• Reprinted together under the title *Evangelicals and the Miraculous*

Fellowship of Word and Spirit is a registered charity, no. 293159

A list of all our publications and resources may be found at
<u>www.fows.org</u>